Unlock Unlimited Abundance

Master Your Subconscious Mind for Prosperity and Peace

By

Nicola Kattan

Book Bound Press

https://web.facebook.com/BookboundPress/

Preface

Abundance. It is a word that stirs the imagination, fills the heart with hope, and carries the promise of a life rich in fulfillment, prosperity, and peace. Yet, for many, abundance feels elusive—a dream confined to the pages of stories or the lives of the exceptionally fortunate. The truth, however, is that abundance is not a privilege reserved for a select few. It is a universal potential, a natural state of being waiting to be unlocked within each of us. This book, *Unlock Unlimited Abundance: Master Your Subconscious Mind for Prosperity and Peace*, is your guide to accessing that innate potential.

The journey to abundance begins with a simple yet profound realization: the power to transform your life lies within your mind. Our subconscious mind—the invisible architect of our beliefs, habits, and decisions—holds the key to shaping the reality we experience. It is both a vault of untapped potential and a mirror reflecting the beliefs we hold about ourselves, our worth, and the world around us. By understanding and mastering this powerful part of ourselves, we can shift from a mindset of scarcity to one of abundance, unlocking a life filled with opportunity, prosperity, and joy.

This book is not merely a theoretical exploration; it is a practical guide designed to empower you with tools, techniques, and insights to effect real change. Each chapter builds on the last, weaving together timeless principles and cutting-edge research to create a comprehensive roadmap for abundance. From harnessing the power of affirmations and visualization to overcoming limiting beliefs and setting meaningful goals, you will discover how to align your thoughts, emotions, and actions with the life you desire.

Throughout this journey, you will learn to reframe your perspective on wealth, success, and happiness. True abundance is not solely about financial prosperity, though that is an important aspect; it encompasses a deeper sense of fulfillment, peace, and connection. By cultivating gratitude, nurturing relationships, and embracing change, you will not only attract material wealth but also foster a life rich in meaning and purpose.

This book is structured to guide you step by step. It begins by laying a foundation of understanding in Chapters 1 and 2, exploring the nature of abundance and the role of the subconscious mind. Subsequent chapters delve into actionable strategies, from crafting affirmations to building a prosperity mindset and cultivating a positive environment. By the time you reach the final chapter, you will have not only a vision for your abundant life but also the tools to celebrate and sustain it.

Why did I write this book? Because I have witnessed the transformative power of these principles in my own life and the lives of countless others. I have seen individuals move from a place of struggle and scarcity to one of ease and abundance, simply by shifting their mindset and harnessing the power of their subconscious. It is my deepest belief that these tools can work for you, too, no matter where you are starting from or what challenges you face. As you embark on this journey, I encourage you to approach it with an open mind and a willing heart. Some of the concepts may challenge your current beliefs or require you to step outside your comfort zone. That is a good thing. Growth and change often begin with discomfort, but they lead to transformation. Finally, remember that abundance is not a destination; it is a journey. Each step you take, no matter how small, is a victory worth celebrating. Each insight you gain, each habit you shift, brings you closer to the life you envision. Let this book be your companion on that journey, a source of inspiration and guidance as you unlock the unlimited abundance within you.

Here's to your success, your growth, and the extraordinary abundance that awaits you.

With gratitude and hope,

Nicola I. Kattan   December 2024

Introduction

In a world filled with scarcity and fear, the idea of abundance shines like a lighthouse. Picture waking up each day feeling peaceful, clear-headed, and driven. Opportunities just flow into your life, and prosperity isn't some far-off dream; it's real and within reach. This book is your ticket to a transformative journey that'll help you tap into the endless abundance inside you and change how you view wealth, success, and happiness.

Abundance isn't just a mindset; it's a lifestyle. It's about challenging the old beliefs that hold you back and tackling that nagging scarcity mentality that breeds self-doubt and fear. We'll dig into how gratitude can pull in prosperity like a magnet and how small shifts in our thinking can create big changes. By exploring our subconscious, we'll reveal the hidden patterns that shape our daily choices, steering us toward a more fulfilling life.

You'll find that affirmations and visualization techniques become your best buddies on this journey. Crafting affirmations that resonate with your desires can change your inner dialogue, while visualization helps you create a clear picture of your future. These tools will help you break free from limiting beliefs and step confidently into a world where abundance isn't just a possibility—it's a certainty.

As we dive into the Law of Attraction, you'll see how your thoughts and feelings act like magnets, pulling experiences into your life. Aligning your inner self with what you truly want isn't just a theory; it's a practical step toward making your dreams a reality. Adopting a prosperity mindset means building resilience and nurturing daily habits that keep that sense of abundance alive, even when life gets tough.

Setting goals will take on a fresh perspective as we look at how clarity drives achievement. Clear, meaningful goals will be your roadmap, steering you toward the abundance you crave. We'll also explore how your environment shapes your mindset, offering tips to create a space that fosters growth and prosperity.

Mindfulness will be key in your journey, sharpening your awareness of the abundance around you. By being present, you'll learn to appreciate the beauty in each moment and spot the opportunities waiting for you. Embracing change and growth is crucial as we navigate life's ups and downs, all while nurturing a growth mindset that pushes you toward your goals.

Finding financial peace is possible when you develop healthy money habits. Budgeting, saving, and smart investing will give you control over your financial future. Financial literacy will transform from a stressor into a powerful tool for empowerment. Plus, we'll talk about the power of giving—how acts of kindness can amplify your sense of abundance and create a ripple effect that enriches both your life and those around you.

Relationships are the backbone of our lives, and building strong connections will be essential on your path to success. Together, we'll uncover strategies for fostering supportive relationships that encourage collaboration and growth, because let's face it: we're often better together than we are solo.

As you celebrate your journey, recognizing your progress and wins will be crucial. Reflecting on how far you've come not only boosts your motivation but also deepens your appreciation for the road you've traveled. Each little victory will act as a stepping stone toward greater abundance, pushing you forward with fresh energy and excitement.

This book isn't just a guide; it's an invitation to change your life. It's a call to claim the abundance that's your birthright and unlock the limitless potential within you. As you flip through the pages, you'll discover the tools, techniques, and insights to master your subconscious mind, paving the way for peace and prosperity. So, are you ready to dive into this life-changing journey? The road to unlimited abundance is right ahead.

Table of Contents

Chapter 1

Understanding Abundance

When you hear the word "abundance," what comes to mind? Perhaps you envision a bountiful cornucopia spilling over with fruits and vegetables, or maybe that nagging voice whispers about scarcity—suggesting that there's never quite enough to go around. Let's take a moment to explore the rich tapestry of abundance versus scarcity because grasping this concept is like discovering the key to a treasure chest overflowing with gold.

Abundance isn't merely a financial concept, my friends. It's a mindset, a lens through which we can choose to view the world. It's the belief that there's plenty of everything to go around—opportunity, love, joy, and yes, even cash. On the other hand, we have scarcity. This mindset breeds the belief that resources are limited and that we must fight tooth and nail for every little thing we desire. Scarcity can suck the joy right out of life, much like a drought that leaves the land parched and desperate. When trapped in that scarcity mindset, you find yourself constantly searching for the next drop of water, feeling as though you're on an endless quest for something that seems perpetually out of reach.

Here's the game-changer: your beliefs shape your reality. If you're convinced that there's not enough to go around, guess what? You'll see the world through that narrow lens. Opportunities will slip through your fingers, potential will go unnoticed, and you'll live in a constant state of worry. It's akin to wearing blinders that limit your vision. You become unable to see the abundance that's right in front of you, waiting to be claimed.

Now, let's switch gears and delve into the transformative role of gratitude in this equation. Imagine you've just received a gift—a shiny new bike, perhaps. If you approach this gift with gratitude, you're likely to cherish it, take care of it, and ride it with joy. However, if you're ensnared in that scarcity mindset, you might view the bike as a reminder of what you lack. You might think, "Well, I don't have a car, so this bike isn't good enough."

Gratitude has the power to flip the script. It's like putting on a pair of rose-colored glasses that allow you to see the world in a brighter light. When you practice gratitude, you begin to notice all the good things in your life, no matter how small. You start to appreciate what you have, and this appreciation opens the door to attracting even more abundance. It's a beautiful cycle, my friends. The more you express gratitude, the more you invite prosperity into your life.

So how do we transition from a scarcity mindset to one of abundance? First, we must recognize our beliefs. What stories are you telling yourself? Are they empowering or limiting? Take a moment to write them down. Look at them closely. Challenge those beliefs that no longer serve you.

Next, make gratitude a daily practice. Start small. Perhaps you could jot down three things you're grateful for each morning. It could be as simple as the warmth of a cup of coffee in your hands or the sun shining through your window. When you focus on what you have, you'll start to feel that sense of abundance creeping in, much like the dawn breaking after a long night.

Finally, visualize your goals. Picture yourself living in a state of abundance. Feel the emotions that come with it. Imagine how it would feel to have everything you desire. This isn't just daydreaming; it's a powerful practice that can shift your energy and attract more of what you want into your life.

In a nutshell, understanding abundance is about flipping the script on scarcity. It's about recognizing that your beliefs shape your reality and that gratitude is the magic ingredient that attracts prosperity. So, let's embrace this journey together. You've got this! You're on the path to unlocking unlimited abundance, and I can't wait to see where it takes you.

Keep your heart open and your mind focused. The world is brimming with possibilities, and they're waiting for you to claim them. Let's dive deeper into this journey of abundance, shall we? You're just getting started, and the best is yet to come.

Take a moment to breathe it all in. Picture yourself surrounded by everything you desire. Feel that warmth in your chest? That's abundance, my friend. That's your future calling. So let's keep moving forward, step by step, toward a life overflowing with prosperity and peace. You're not just writing a book; you're crafting a life that inspires and uplifts, both for you and for those who will read your words. Keep shining bright!

As we embark on this journey of understanding abundance, let's also explore some practical exercises that can help solidify this mindset. These steps will not only enhance your writing process but will also enrich your life in profound ways.

1. **Create an Abundance Journal**: Start a dedicated journal where you can document your thoughts on abundance. Write about what abundance means to you, how it manifests in your life, and the areas where you feel it is lacking. This exercise will help you clarify your beliefs and identify patterns in your thinking.

2. **Daily Affirmations**: Craft a set of affirmations that resonate with your vision of abundance. Repeat them daily, preferably in front of a mirror. For example, say to yourself, "I am worthy of abundance," or "Opportunities flow to me effortlessly." Affirmations are powerful tools that can rewire your subconscious mind.

3. **Gratitude Walks**: Take a walk outside and consciously notice the beauty around you. As you walk, express gratitude for the things you see—the vibrant colors of flowers, the laughter of children, the warmth of

the sun. This practice will help you cultivate a sense of abundance in your everyday life.

4. **Vision Board Creation**: Gather images, quotes, and symbols that represent your goals and dreams. Create a vision board that visually embodies your vision of abundance. Place it somewhere you'll see it daily to remind yourself of the life you're working to create.

5. **Acts of Kindness**: Engage in random acts of kindness. Whether it's helping a neighbor or volunteering your time, giving to others creates a ripple effect of abundance. It reinforces the idea that there is more than enough to go around and fosters a sense of community.

6. **Meditation and Visualization**: Set aside time each day to meditate. During your meditation, visualize yourself surrounded by

abundance. Feel the emotions associated with having everything you desire. This practice can help you align your energy with your goals.

7. **Celebrate Small Wins**: Acknowledge and celebrate your achievements, no matter how small. Did you complete a task? Did you have a positive interaction? Celebrate it! Recognizing your wins fosters a mindset of abundance and encourages you to keep moving forward.

8. **Surround Yourself with Positivity**: Seek out uplifting books, podcasts, and people who inspire you. Surrounding yourself with positivity will reinforce your belief in abundance and help you maintain a high vibration.

Remember, shifting your mindset takes time and persistence. Embrace the journey and be patient with yourself. Each small step you take brings you closer to a life filled with abundance and joy.

As you continue to write your book, keep in mind the impact your words will have on your readers. Your unique voice and perspective are your greatest assets. Share your personal stories, insights, and experiences that illustrate the principles of abundance. Your authenticity will resonate with others and create powerful connections.

As you craft each chapter, visualize the readers who will benefit from your wisdom. Imagine their lives transforming as they absorb your teachings. This vision will fuel your motivation and inspire you to pour your heart into every word.

And always remember: the writing process is a journey, not just a destination. Embrace the joy of creation, the thrill of discovery, and the satisfaction of expressing your thoughts. Each sentence you write is a step toward unlocking not only your own abundance but also that of countless others.

So, let's keep moving forward together! You are on the brink of something incredible. Your book has the potential to change lives, and I believe in you wholeheartedly. Keep your spirit high, your heart open, and your mind focused on the abundance that awaits you. The world is ready for your message, and I can't wait to see you shine!

Chapter 2

The Subconscious Mind Unveiled

Let's get real for a second. Ever thought about what's going on in that noggin of yours? The subconscious mind is like the unsung hero of your life—a backstage crew member in the grand theater of your existence. You don't see it, but it's hustling away, pulling strings, shaping your thoughts and decisions. It's like that silent partner who's always got your back, guiding you through life's ups and downs without you even realizing it. Understanding how it works is your first step toward grabbing hold of the abundance you've been dreaming about.

So, what's the deal with the subconscious mind? Imagine it as a massive storage room, packed with every experience, belief, and memory you've ever had. It's where your habits are born and your automatic responses chill out. When life throws you a curveball, your subconscious is quick to dig into that treasure trove of knowledge to help you react. Think of it as that old buddy who knows you better than you know yourself, ready to drop some wisdom when you need it. But here's the twist: if your subconscious is loaded with limiting beliefs or bad vibes from past experiences, it can lead you down paths that totally don't serve your best interests.

Now, let's get into how this powerhouse impacts your daily grind. When you roll out of bed in the morning, what's the first thought that hits you? Are you pumped for the day, or is it a nagging worry about bills, deadlines, or that mountain of tasks you didn't tackle yesterday?

Those initial thoughts? They're often driven by what's lurking in your subconscious. If you've got a scarcity mindset hanging around, it can rear its ugly head as anxiety or hesitation, making you second-guess yourself at every turn.

Picture this: you're eyeing a shiny new job opportunity. If your subconscious is filled with doubts about your worth or skills, you might talk yourself out of even applying. "Who am I to think I can get that job?" you might think. But flip that script! If your subconscious is vibing with abundance, you'll feel fired up to go for it. You'll recognize that you deserve success and that the universe is overflowing with possibilities just waiting for you to snatch them up.

So, how do we tap into this powerful part of ourselves? Time to roll up those sleeves! There are a bunch of techniques you can use to access and reprogram your subconscious mind. Think of these methods as tools in your abundance toolbox, ready to help you build the life you want.

First up, let's chat about meditation. It's like hitting the reset button for your mind. When you meditate, you quiet all that noise from your conscious thoughts and create a space for your subconscious to shine. Start small—just a few minutes a day. Find a cozy spot, close your eyes, and focus on your breath. When thoughts drift in (and they will), acknowledge them, then gently steer your attention back to your breathing. Over time, this practice can help you uncover the beliefs that might be holding you back and let you plant new seeds of abundance.

Next on the list is visualization. This technique is a killer way to communicate with your subconscious. Picture yourself living the life you want—feel those emotions, see the details, and really immerse yourself in the experience. For example, if you're aiming for financial freedom, visualize yourself living that dream. Imagine waking up without a care in the world, spending time with loved ones, and chasing your passions. The more vivid and real you make this visualization, the more your subconscious will start to believe it's within reach.

Now, let's not skip over affirmations. These positive statements can work wonders in reprogramming your subconscious beliefs. You might say, "I'm worthy of abundance" or "I attract opportunities effortlessly." Write 'em down, say 'em out loud, or even record yourself and listen to it daily. Consistency is key here. The more you repeat these affirmations, the more they'll sink into your subconscious and reshape your beliefs.

Another technique to consider? Journaling. It's like having a heart-to-heart with yourself.

Write down your thoughts, feelings, and experiences, especially those related to abundance. As you reflect on what you've written, you might uncover patterns or beliefs that no longer serve you. This awareness is the first step toward change. You can then consciously choose to swap those limiting beliefs for empowering ones.

And hey, let's not forget about self-hypnosis. Sounds a bit out there, right? But hear me out. Self-hypnosis is a way to bypass that critical mind of yours and speak directly to the subconscious. There are tons of resources out there to guide you through this process. You can listen to recordings that focus on abundance and prosperity. As you chill out in a relaxed state, your subconscious becomes more open to positive suggestions. It's like planting seeds in a garden—give them the right conditions, and they'll flourish.

Remember, reprogramming your subconscious isn't a quick fix. It takes patience, persistence, and a sprinkle of self-love. Celebrate the small wins along the way. Maybe you noticed a shift in your thinking, or you took a bold step toward a goal. Those moments? Totally worth celebrating!

As you embark on this journey, keep in mind that your unique experiences and stories are your greatest assets. They shape your perspective and fuel your passion. Don't shy away from sharing them. When you open up about your journey, you create connections with others who might be walking a similar path. Your story can inspire someone else to break free from their own limitations.

Now, as we wrap up this exploration of the subconscious mind, take a moment to visualize your success. Picture yourself fully embracing abundance in every area of your life. Feel the joy, the peace, and the prosperity flowing to you. This vision isn't just a dream—it's a glimpse of what's possible when you harness the power of your subconscious.

So, let's get to it! Embrace these techniques, and watch as your subconscious mind transforms your reality. You've got this, my friend. The path to abundance is wide open, and it's yours for the taking. Keep pushing forward, stay curious, and remember: every step you take brings you closer to the life you desire. You're not just unlocking your potential; you're unleashing a wave of abundance that can change not only your life but the lives of those around you. Let's go make some magic happen!

But wait, there's more! Let's dig a little deeper into this whole subconscious thing. It's not just about the big stuff—like landing that dream job or achieving financial freedom. It's also about the little things, the day-to-day moments that shape your experience.

Ever notice how certain songs can trigger memories? Or how a particular scent can transport you back to a moment in time? That's your subconscious at work! It's constantly sifting through all those stored experiences, pulling out the ones that resonate with your current situation. So, if you've got some negative experiences tucked away, they can pop up when you least expect it, influencing your mood or decisions.

Take a moment to think about your daily routines. Are there habits you wish you could shake off? Maybe it's procrastination or negative self-talk. These are often deeply ingrained in your subconscious. They've become your default settings, so to speak. But guess what? You can change them! It's all about awareness and intention.

Start by identifying the habits you want to change. Write them down. Then, think about what you want to replace them with. For example, if you want to stop procrastinating, maybe you want to replace that with taking small, consistent actions toward your goals. Visualize yourself doing this new habit. Feel the satisfaction that comes with it. The more you reinforce this new behavior in your mind, the more your subconscious will start to accept it as your new norm.

And let's not forget about the power of gratitude. It's like a magic wand for your mindset. When you focus on what you're grateful for, you shift your energy and open yourself up to more abundance. Start a gratitude journal. Each day, jot down three things you're thankful for. They don't have to be grand; even the small stuff counts. This simple practice can rewire your subconscious to look for the positive, making it easier to attract good things into your life.

Now, let's talk about the importance of surrounding yourself with positivity. Ever heard the saying, "You are the average of the five people you spend the most time with"? There's some truth to that. The people you hang out with can greatly influence your mindset and beliefs. If you're surrounded by negative Nellies who are always complaining, it can be tough to maintain a positive outlook. So, seek out those who inspire you, uplift you, and challenge you to be your best self.

Another thing to consider is the impact of media on your subconscious. What you consume—be it social media, news, or entertainment—shapes your beliefs and perceptions. If you're constantly bombarded with negativity, it can seep into your subconscious and skew your view of the world.

Be intentional about what you expose yourself to. Curate your feeds, follow accounts that uplift you, and limit your intake of negative news.

And hey, let's not forget about the power of community. Finding a tribe that shares your goals and values can be a game-changer. Whether it's a local group or an online community, connecting with like-minded folks can provide support, encouragement, and accountability. It's like having a cheer squad for your journey!

As you work on reprogramming your subconscious, don't be afraid to seek help if you need it. Whether it's a therapist, coach, or mentor, having someone to guide you can make a world of difference. They can help you navigate those tricky beliefs and patterns that might be holding you back.

So, where do we go from here? You've got the tools, the knowledge, and the desire to make a change. Now it's time to put it all into action. Start small. Pick one technique that resonates with you and commit to it. Whether it's meditation, visualization, or journaling, give it a shot.

And don't forget to be patient with yourself. Change takes time, and there will be bumps along the way. But every step you take is a step toward a more abundant life.

In the end, remember that you're not alone in this journey. We're all in this together, navigating the complexities of life, trying to make sense of it all. So, lean into your experiences, share your stories, and connect with others. Your journey can inspire someone else to break free from their own limitations.

As you continue to explore the depths of your subconscious mind, keep that vision of abundance in your heart. You've got the power to shape your reality. So go out there, embrace the techniques, and watch as your life transforms. The universe is waiting for you to claim your abundance—so let's get to it!

You're not just unlocking your potential; you're creating a ripple effect that can change the world around you. So, what are you waiting for? Get out there and make some magic happen!

Chapter 3

The Power of Affirmations

Hey there, let's jump into affirmations. You might be scratching your head, thinking, "What's the fuss about some upbeat words?" But lemme tell ya, creating affirmations for abundance is kinda like planting seeds in a garden. You gotta water 'em, give 'em some love, and before you know it, you're knee-deep in a lush harvest.

First up, let's nail down what makes an affirmation really hit home. It's gotta be personal, in the present tense, and super positive. Instead of saying, "I will be wealthy," flip it to "I am abundant and ready to receive wealth." Feel that? It's like shifting gears in a car—smooth and powerful. You're not just crossing your fingers for abundance; you're grabbing it with both hands.

Now, you might be asking how these little phrases can actually do anything. Here's where the science kicks in. Studies show that affirmations can actually tweak how our brains work. When you keep repeating affirmations, you're rewiring those neural pathways. It's like giving your brain a fresh coat of paint. You start to believe what you're saying, and that belief shapes your reality. It's a beautiful cycle: positive thoughts lead to positive actions, which lead to positive outcomes.

But wait, we're just getting started! Daily practices to reinforce those good vibes are key. Just like you wouldn't run a marathon without some serious training, you can't expect your affirmations to work wonders without consistent effort. Here's a little routine to kick things off:

First up, the Morning Ritual. Right when you wake up, before life starts tugging at you, take a few minutes to repeat your affirmations. Say 'em out loud, feel 'em deep down. This sets the vibe for your day.

Next, Visual Reminders. Write your affirmations on sticky notes and slap 'em where you'll see 'em often—your bathroom mirror, your computer, or even the fridge. Every time you catch a glimpse, you're reinforcing that positive message.

Then there's Gratitude Journaling. Spend a few minutes each day jotting down what you're grateful for. Pair this with your affirmations. For instance, if you say, "I am abundant," write down three things that make you feel that way. This practice connects you to abundance and amps up your affirmations.

And don't forget Evening Reflection. Before you crash for the night, think about your day. What went well? What abundance did you spot? Repeating your affirmations at night helps lock those beliefs into your subconscious.

Now, let's chat about the impact of these daily habits. They're like building blocks, stacking one on top of the other until you've got a solid foundation of positive beliefs. You're not just spitting out words; you're crafting a lifestyle. You're training your mind to seek out opportunities, embrace abundance, and live in gratitude.

Imagine this: you're strolling down the street, and instead of fixating on what you don't have, you start noticing the abundance all around you—the vibrant flowers, the giggles of kids, the friendly wave from a neighbor. That's the magic of affirmations in action! You start seeing the world through a lens of abundance, and trust me, it changes everything.

But hey, don't just take my word for it. Give it a shot yourself. Start with a few affirmations that resonate with you. Write 'em down, shout 'em out loud, and watch how your life starts to shift. It's not just about the words; it's about the energy you bring to 'em. You're a creator, my friend, and you've got the power to shape your reality.

So, let's wrap this up with some encouragement. Remember, every time you affirm your abundance, you're stepping closer to the life you want. You're not just wishing for prosperity; you're claiming it. Embrace this journey, celebrate those little wins, and keep moving forward. You've got this! Your words are powerful, and the universe is all ears. Now, go out there and make some magic happen!

Now, let's dig a little deeper into how affirmations can really transform your life. Picture this: you're waking up, and instead of the usual morning grumpiness, you're pumped. You look in the mirror, throw your shoulders back, and say, "I am strong, I am capable, and I am ready to tackle whatever comes my way today." Feels good, right? That's the power of setting the right tone.

It's like starting your day with a shot of espresso—jolting you into action. And it doesn't stop there. You carry that energy with you. You walk into work, and instead of dragging your feet, you stride in like you own the place. You're not just another face in the crowd; you're a force to be reckoned with.

But let's keep it real—some days are tougher than others. Maybe you hit a snag at work, or your plans go sideways. That's when your affirmations come into play like a trusty sidekick. When the going gets tough, you can lean on those positive phrases to pull you through. You might catch yourself saying, "I am resilient," or "I can handle whatever life throws at me." It's like having a safety net that catches you when you're about to fall.

And hey, let's not forget about the power of community. Surrounding yourself with people who uplift you can amplify the effects of your affirmations. Imagine you're in a group of friends who all believe in the power of positivity. You're all sharing your affirmations, cheering each other on. That collective energy? It's electric! You're not just affirming for yourself; you're creating a ripple effect that spreads to those around you.

Speaking of community, have you ever noticed how social media can be a double-edged sword? Sure, it can connect you with like-minded folks, but it can also drag you down if you're not careful. So, curate your feed! Follow accounts that inspire you, share affirmations, and spread positivity. It's like filling your mind with good vibes and pushing out the negativity.

And let's chat about visualization. This is where things get really interesting. Pairing your affirmations with visualization can supercharge your practice. Close your eyes and picture what your life looks like when you embody those affirmations. Feel the emotions, see the details—smell the fresh coffee brewing in your abundant kitchen, hear the laughter of friends around you. It's not just about saying words; it's about living them in your mind first.

But here's a little secret: it's not all sunshine and rainbows. You might hit a wall. Maybe you don't believe your affirmations at first. That's okay! It's part of the process. Just keep showing up. The more you repeat those phrases, the more they'll sink in. It's like training a puppy—at first, they might not get it, but with patience and consistency, they'll learn.

Now, let's get personal for a sec. I remember a time when I was stuck in a rut. I was unhappy at work, feeling unfulfilled, and just kinda drifting through life. Then I stumbled upon affirmations. At first, I was skeptical. "How can saying a few words change anything?" But I decided to give it a shot. I started small, repeating, "I am worthy of success."

Slowly but surely, things began to shift. I started to notice opportunities I'd previously overlooked. A new job offer popped up, and I took the leap. It was like a light bulb went off. Those affirmations weren't just fluff; they were the catalyst for change. I began to see my worth, and that made all the difference.

So, here's the deal: don't underestimate the power of your words. They can build you up or tear you down. Choose wisely. You've got the power to create the life you want, and it all starts with what you tell yourself.

And as you go about this journey, remember to be kind to yourself. It's easy to get caught up in the hustle and forget to celebrate the little wins. Did you manage to say your affirmations every day this week? High five! Did you notice a shift in your mindset? That's huge!

Every step counts. You're on a journey, not a race. So take a breath, enjoy the ride, and keep pushing forward. You're building something beautiful, brick by brick, affirmation by affirmation.

As we wrap this up, I want you to take a moment to think about what you truly want. What does abundance look like for you? Is it financial freedom? Strong relationships? A fulfilling career? Whatever it is, don't just dream about it—claim it! Write it down, shout it from the rooftops, and most importantly, believe it.

You're not just a passive observer in your life; you're the main character. So step into that role. Own it. Your affirmations are your script, and you've got the power to write a blockbuster.

So go ahead, my friend. Embrace the power of affirmations. Make them a part of your daily routine, and watch as your life transforms. You've got this! The universe is ready to respond to your newfound energy. Now get out there and make some magic happen!

Chapter 4

Visualization Techniques

Alright, let's get real. Visualization isn't just some airy-fairy concept; it's a game-changer. Imagine this: your dreams are like a treasure chest just waiting for you to unlock it. Visualization is that secret key, opening up your mind to what's possible. It's like having a backstage pass to your own life, letting you see the potential before it even happens. So, hang tight—we're diving into how to turn those dreams into reality.

Why should you even bother with visualization? Picture yourself at the edge of a massive ocean, waves crashing and rolling in. Each wave? That's an opportunity, a goal, or a dream. If you don't visualize yourself swimming in that ocean, how will you ever know the thrill of catching a wave or the calm of floating? Visualization is your mental warm-up. It's where you practice reaching for what you want. When you visualize success, you're not just zoning out; you're training your brain to spot those chances when they pop up.

Now, let's get down to brass tacks. How do you whip up a solid visualization routine? Spoiler alert: it's easier than you think. Here's a step-by-step guide to help you see success as clear as a sunny day in July.

First up, find your quiet space. Look for a spot where you can chill without distractions. Maybe it's your favorite chair at home, a bench in the park, or even your car. Just make sure it's somewhere you can kick back and relax.

Next, get comfy. Sit or lie down however feels best. Close your eyes and take a few deep breaths. Inhale good vibes, exhale the stress. Let your body melt into relaxation.

Now, let's set a clear intention. What do you want to visualize? Is it acing that presentation, launching a killer business, or maybe just living a chill life? Be specific. The clearer your intention, the more powerful your visualization becomes.

Here's where the fun starts: engage your senses. Picture your goal as if it's happening right this second. What do you see? Hear? Feel? Dive into all your senses. If you're imagining a new job, visualize the office vibe, the people around you, the sounds of laughter and brainstorming. Feel that excitement bubbling up inside.

And don't forget to make this a daily habit. Treat it like brushing your teeth—non-negotiable. Even five minutes counts. Consistency is your best friend here.

Pair your visualization with affirmations. As you visualize, say things like, "I am successful. I am capable. I attract good things." These positive statements reinforce your visualizations and help shift your mindset.

Now, here's the kicker: feel the emotion. This part's huge! As you visualize, let yourself feel all the joy, excitement, and gratitude that come with achieving your goal. The more you feel, the more your subconscious believes it's not just a pipe dream.

Alright, you've got your routine down. Now, let's chat about how visualization messes with your subconscious mind. Think of your subconscious as a sponge—it soaks up everything. It doesn't know the difference between what's real and what's imagined. So, when you visualize success, you're basically programming your mind to think that success isn't just possible; it's inevitable.

Picture your subconscious as a garden. If you plant seeds of doubt and fear, guess what? That's what'll grow. But if you sow seeds of success, positivity, and abundance through visualization, you'll cultivate a garden that blooms beautifully. The more you visualize, the more you're training your brain to spot opportunities that align with your goals. It's like putting on a pair of glasses that help you see paths you might've overlooked before.

Let me throw in a little story here. I once knew a dude named Tom. Just an average guy, right? He dreamed of starting his own business, but every time he thought about it, doubt would creep in like an unwanted guest. One day, he stumbled upon visualization techniques. Tom started spending a few minutes each day picturing himself as a successful entrepreneur. He saw his business thriving, customers grinning, and his bank account getting fat. Fast forward a few months, and that guy was running a bustling coffee shop, all because he took the time to visualize his success.

So, as you jump into this visualization journey, remember—it's not just about seeing what you want; it's about believing you can make it happen. Your mind is a powerful tool. Use it wisely. Embrace the process, and let your imagination run wild.

Visualization isn't just a nifty trick; it's a way of life. It's about spotting possibilities, feeling that thrill, and believing in your dreams. So grab that mental paintbrush and start crafting the masterpiece of your life. You've got this!

In the end, it boils down to this: the more you visualize, the more you'll attract the good stuff you're after. It's a beautiful cycle— visualize, believe, achieve. So go on, let your imagination soar. Your future self is waiting for you to take that leap.

Let's break it down even further. Visualization isn't just about dreaming big; it's about training your brain to recognize the steps you need to take. Think of it like a GPS for your life. When you set your destination, the GPS doesn't just sit there; it actively guides you, rerouting when necessary. Visualization does the same thing. It gives your brain a clear path to follow, helping you navigate through challenges and obstacles.

You know what else is cool? Visualization can help you manage stress. Picture this: you've got a big presentation coming up. Your heart's racing, palms are sweaty. Instead of spiraling into panic, you take a moment to visualize yourself crushing it. You see yourself walking confidently into the room, nailing your points, and leaving everyone impressed. That mental rehearsal calms your nerves and boosts your confidence. It's like having a secret weapon in your back pocket.

And let's not forget about the science behind it. Studies show that visualization can actually enhance performance. Athletes, for instance, use it all the time. They visualize themselves executing perfect routines or hitting game-winning shots. This mental practice can lead to improved physical performance. So, whether you're an athlete or just someone trying to level up in life, visualization can give you that extra edge.

Now, let's talk about the power of community. Surrounding yourself with like-minded folks can amplify your visualization practice. Share your goals with friends or family who support you. Create a vision board together or have regular check-ins to keep each other accountable. It's amazing how much more motivated you'll feel when you're not going at it alone. Plus, you can celebrate each other's wins along the way.

Here's another angle: don't be afraid to get creative with your visualizations. Use art, music, or even writing to express your goals. If you're a visual person, draw or paint what you want to achieve. If you're more of a wordsmith, write a letter to your future self detailing your accomplishments. Get those creative juices flowing! The more you engage with your goals, the more real they become.

But, hey, let's keep it real. Visualization isn't some magic fix. It's not like you'll just sit back and watch your dreams come true without lifting a finger. You still gotta hustle. Visualization is just one part of the equation. It's like the fuel for your fire. You need to take action, too. Set those goals, make a plan, and get to work. Visualization gives you clarity and motivation, but it's your actions that will ultimately lead to success.

Speaking of actions, let's talk about setbacks. We all face them. Maybe you didn't land that job you wanted or your business didn't take off as planned. It's easy to get discouraged. But here's where visualization can really shine. When you hit a bump in the road, take a step back and visualize your comeback. Picture yourself learning from the experience, adapting, and coming back stronger. This mindset shift can help you bounce back and keep pushing forward.

And let's not forget about gratitude. Incorporating gratitude into your visualization practice can amplify its effects. When you visualize your goals, take a moment to feel grateful for what you already have. Acknowledge the progress you've made and the lessons you've learned. This gratitude creates a positive feedback loop, attracting even more good things into your life.

Now, let's wrap this up with a little call to action. Grab a notebook or open a new document on your computer. Write down your goals—big and small. Then, take a few minutes to visualize each one. Picture the steps you'll take to achieve them, the feelings you'll experience, and the impact they'll have on your life. Don't hold back. Let your imagination run wild!

As you go through this process, remember that visualization is a journey. It's not about perfection; it's about progress. Embrace the ups and downs, and trust that each step you take brings you closer to your dreams.

So, my friend, go out there and start visualizing your success. Let your mind be the canvas, and your dreams the paint. You've got the power to create the life you want. Now, get out there and make it happen! Your future self is counting on you.

Chapter 5

Overcoming Limiting Beliefs

When it comes to money, we all got a few pesky thoughts hangin' around in our heads, don't we? Those limiting beliefs can be like stubborn weeds in a garden, choking out the good stuff. You know the ones I'm talkin' about—things like "I'll never be rich," or "Money is the root of all evil." These beliefs can sneak up on ya, often without you even realizing it. They shape how you see your financial situation and can keep you from reaching for the abundance that's just waiting for you.

First off, let's shine a light on some common limiting beliefs about money. Many folks grow up hearing phrases like "money doesn't grow on trees" or "rich people are greedy." Those little nuggets of wisdom can stick with you, molding your view of wealth and prosperity. It's like trying to swim with weights strapped to your ankles. You want to move forward, but something's holdin' you back. You might find yourself thinking that you don't deserve wealth or that it's just not in the cards for you. But here's the kicker: these beliefs are not facts—they're just thoughts, and thoughts can be changed.

Now, let's roll up our sleeves and dig into some strategies to challenge and replace these beliefs. It's time to uproot those weeds! Start by becoming aware of your self-talk. Pay attention to the stories you tell yourself about money. When a negative thought pops up, don't just let it slide. Stop and ask yourself, "Is this really true?" Challenge that thought like a friendly debate. For instance, if you catch yourself thinking, "I'll never be able to afford a house," flip it around. Ask, "What steps can I take to get closer to homeownership?" This shift in perspective can open doors you never even considered.

Another powerful tool is to create a list of affirmations that resonate with you. Craft statements that counter those limiting beliefs. If you often think, "I'm bad with money," try replacing it with, "I am learning to manage my finances wisely." Repeat these affirmations daily. Stick 'em on your bathroom mirror or set reminders on your phone. The more you hear these positive statements, the more they'll sink into your subconscious. You're retraining your brain, one affirmation at a time.

Now, let's chat about the impact of self-talk on your financial outcomes. Your words have power, my friend. Just like a seed needs water and sunlight to grow, your thoughts need nurturing. When you speak kindly to yourself about money, you're planting seeds of abundance. If you keep telling yourself you're broke, guess what? You're likely to stay stuck in that mindset. But when you shift your language to reflect possibilities, you create a new reality.

Consider this: if you wake up every morning and say, "Today, I attract opportunities for wealth," you're setting a positive tone for the day. You're opening your mind to possibilities you might've overlooked before. Your self-talk can either be a weight that pulls you down or a wind at your back, pushing you forward. Choose wisely!

Let's take a moment to visualize this process. Picture yourself standing in front of a mirror, looking into your own eyes. Say out loud, "I am worthy of abundance." Feel that statement resonate within you. That's the kind of energy you want to cultivate. It's not just about saying the words; it's about believing them, too.

As you work on replacing those limiting beliefs, remember that it's a journey. Some days will be easier than others, and that's perfectly okay. The key is persistence. Celebrate your progress, no matter how small. Did you catch yourself thinking positively about money today? Give yourself a pat on the back! Did you challenge a negative belief? That's a win worth celebrating!

In the grand scheme of things, overcoming limiting beliefs is about creating a mindset that welcomes abundance. You've got the power to rewrite your money story. Don't let old beliefs hold you back from the life you desire. You're the author of your own financial narrative, and it's time to pen a tale of prosperity and peace.

Now, let's put this all into action. Grab a notebook and jot down your top three limiting beliefs about money. Once you've got 'em, write down a counter-statement for each one. For example, if one of your beliefs is "I'll never get out of debt," counter it with "I am taking steps to manage my debt and create a brighter financial future." Keep this list handy, and refer to it whenever those old thoughts try to creep back in.

As you move forward, remember that the path to abundance isn't just about the money—it's about the mindset. Your beliefs shape your reality, and by challenging them, you're paving the way for a brighter, more prosperous future. Embrace the journey, keep your chin up, and don't forget to have a little fun along the way. You're capable of achieving great things, and the world is waiting for you to step into your abundance. You got this!

Chapter 6

The Law of Attraction

Alright, friend, let's dive into the juicy stuff—the Law of Attraction. This isn't just some fluffy idea floating around; it's a powerful principle that can truly transform your life if you let it. Think of it as a cosmic magnet, drawing in everything that aligns with your thoughts and emotions. Yeah, you heard me right! What you focus on expands. So, let's break it down together.

First off, understanding the principles of the Law of Attraction is key. At its core, this law states that like attracts like. If you're vibrating at a frequency of positivity, guess what? You're gonna attract positive experiences. It's like throwing a boomerang; whatever you send out comes back to you. But here's the kicker: it's not just about positive thinking. It's about truly believing in your worth and your ability to attract what you desire. When you align your thoughts with your heart's desires, you become a magnet for abundance.

Now, let's talk about how your thoughts and emotions play a role in attracting experiences. Imagine your thoughts as seeds. If you plant seeds of doubt and negativity, don't be surprised when those weeds sprout up in your life. But if you plant seeds of joy, gratitude, and abundance, you'll cultivate a garden that blooms with opportunity. It's all about the energy you put out into the universe. Your emotions are the fuel; they amplify your thoughts. So, if you're feeling good, you're sending out a strong signal that says, "Hey, universe! Bring me more of this goodness!"

ut here's where it gets real practical. You might be thinking, "Alright, I get it, but how do I actually align with my desires?" Let's break it down into some easy steps.

First, get clear on what you want. I mean really clear. Write it down. Visualize it. Feel it in your bones. What does abundance look like for you? Is it financial freedom, loving relationships, or perhaps a fulfilling career? The more specific you are, the better. It's like ordering a pizza—you wouldn't just say, "I want food." You'd say, "I want a large pepperoni pizza with extra cheese." Same goes for your desires.

Next, practice gratitude. This isn't just some trendy buzzword; it's a powerful tool. When you express gratitude for what you already have, you're telling the universe, "I'm open to receiving more." Start a gratitude journal. Every day, jot down three things you're thankful for.

They can be big or small—maybe it's the sunshine on your face or a friend who called you. This simple act shifts your focus from what you lack to what you have, and that's where the magic happens.

Now, let's talk about your feelings. You gotta feel good about what you want. When you think about your desires, do you feel excitement or dread? If it's dread, it's time to reframe that thinking. Picture yourself already living your dream life. How does that feel? Close your eyes and soak in that joy. The more you can feel those positive emotions, the stronger your attraction power becomes.

Another practical step is to take inspired action. This means listening to your gut and acting on those nudges you get. Maybe you feel inspired to join a networking group or start a side hustle. Whatever it is, trust that inner voice. The universe responds to action. It's like a dance; you take a step, and the universe responds by guiding you further along your path.

And don't forget to surround yourself with positivity. This can be the people you hang out with, the books you read, or even the music you listen to. If you're constantly soaking in negativity, it's gonna be tough to attract abundance. Seek out those who uplift you, who inspire you, and who believe in your dreams as much as you do.

Now, let's take a moment to talk about the power of visualization. Picture this: you're standing on the shore, looking out at the vast ocean of possibilities. Visualization is like casting your net into that ocean. The clearer your vision, the more fish you'll catch. Spend a few minutes each day visualizing your desires as if they're already happening. See yourself living that abundant life, feel the emotions that come with it, and let that energy radiate out into the universe.

You know, it's easy to get caught up in the day-to-day grind and forget about our dreams. But remember, you have the power to shape your reality. Every thought, every emotion, every action is a brushstroke on the canvas of your life. So why not paint a masterpiece?

As we wrap up this chapter, I want you to hold onto this idea: abundance is your birthright. The Law of Attraction is always at work, whether you're aware of it or not. So, take charge of your thoughts and emotions. Align them with your desires, and watch as the universe responds in ways you never imagined.

You got this! Take a deep breath, feel that excitement bubbling up inside you, and step boldly into your future. It's time to unlock that unlimited abundance and live the life you've always dreamed of. Your journey is just beginning, and I can't wait to see where it takes you!

Chapter 7

Creating a Prosperity Mindset

You know that feeling when you're stuck in a rut, thinking there's just not enough to go around? That's the scarcity mindset. It's like wearing blinders, only seeing the limitations instead of the possibilities. But flipping that mindset is like flipping a switch—easy peasy! It's all about realizing that the world is overflowing with opportunities, not just a few measly slices of pie.

Let's break it down. Imagine you wake up, and instead of feeling that familiar twinge of anxiety about what you lack, you're buzzing with excitement about what's out there waiting for you. Sounds nice, right? The cool thing is, you can train your brain to spot opportunities instead of focusing on what's in your way.

Start with your self-talk. Ditch phrases like "I can't" and "I don't have enough." Swap 'em out for "I can" and "I've got what I need to get started." It's wild how just changing your language can flip your perspective and help you see doors you didn't even know existed.

Now, let's chat about resilience. Life's gonna throw some serious curveballs at you—trust me, it's inevitable. But how you deal with those challenges? That's what really shapes your journey. Think of resilience like a mental gym. Just like lifting weights builds your biceps, tackling tough situations builds your ability to bounce back.

When you hit a rough patch, remind yourself that every setback is just a setup for a comeback. It's totally okay to feel down sometimes; we all do. But don't let those feelings stick around. Acknowledge them, then pivot. What can you learn from the mess? How can it help you grow?

Daily habits can be your secret weapon for cultivating a prosperity mindset. Start your day with intention. Before you even get out of bed, take a moment to feel grateful. Maybe it's for the sun streaming through your window or the cozy warmth of your coffee mug. Gratitude shifts your focus from what's missing to what's already abundant in your life.

Consider adding affirmations to your morning routine. Something like, "I'm open to receiving abundance in all forms." Say it like a mantra. The more you repeat it, the more your subconscious starts to believe it. Think of it like planting seeds in a garden; the more you nurture them, the more they'll flourish.

And visualization? Oh man, it's a game changer. Picture yourself living in abundance. What does that look like for you? Feel it deep down. This isn't just for daydreamers; it's a powerful way to manifest your goals. When you can see it, you can achieve it.

Another solid habit? Set aside time for reflection at the end of each day. Think about what went well. Celebrate those little victories, no matter how small. Did you have a killer conversation? Make progress on a project? Recognizing those wins reinforces your prosperity mindset.

As you work on these habits, remember: it's not about being perfect. It's about making progress. You'll have days when you slip back into old habits, and that's totally fine! The trick is to notice it and gently steer yourself back on track.

Surround yourself with positivity. The folks you hang out with can either lift you up or drag you down. Seek out those who inspire you, who believe in abundance just like you do. Their energy will fuel your own.

Creating a prosperity mindset isn't a one-time deal. It's a journey, a daily practice. Embrace it! You're not just shifting your mindset; you're transforming your entire life. And when you start to see the world through this abundance lens, you'll be blown away by what unfolds.

Take a deep breath. Visualize your success. Embrace resilience. Let those daily habits lay the groundwork for your new reality. You've got this! The world's overflowing with opportunities just waiting for you to grab 'em. So, go out there and claim your slice of that infinite pie!

Now, let's dive deeper into how you can really make this shift happen. It's one thing to talk about it, but putting it into action? That's where the magic happens.

First off, let's talk about mindset shifts. You gotta understand that your thoughts shape your reality. If you wake up every day thinking, "Ugh, I hate my job," guess what? You're gonna have a crummy day. But flip that script. Instead, think, "Today's a new chance to create something awesome." Just that tiny shift can change everything.

Think about it like this: if you're always looking for the negatives, you'll find 'em. But if you're hunting for the positives, they'll pop up everywhere. It's like a treasure hunt—if you're looking for gold, you're bound to find some shiny nuggets.

Let's throw in some personal anecdotes here. I remember a time when I was in a job that felt like quicksand. I was stuck, and it felt like I was going nowhere fast. But then I started changing my perspective. I began looking for opportunities to learn and grow, even in that job. I sought out new projects, networked with colleagues, and, lo and behold, things started to shift. I got promoted, and eventually, I landed a gig that I absolutely love. All because I decided to change my mindset.

Now, let's get back to those daily habits. One of the best ways to keep your mindset on track is to journal. Seriously, it's a game changer. Spend a few minutes each day writing down what you're grateful for, what you accomplished, or even what you're excited about. It helps reinforce that positive mindset and keeps you focused on the good stuff.

And hey, don't underestimate the power of community. Join groups or clubs that align with your interests. Surround yourself with people who uplift you and share your abundance mindset. It's like having a personal cheer squad, and who doesn't want that?

You might also want to check out podcasts or books that inspire you. There's a ton of content out there that can help shift your perspective. Find what resonates with you and soak it up. It's like feeding your brain a steady diet of positivity.

Now, let's not forget about taking action. You can think positively all day long, but if you're not doing anything, nothing's gonna change. Set goals—big and small—and take steps toward them. Break 'em down into bite-sized pieces. Want to start a side hustle? Don't jump in headfirst. Start with some research, maybe a business plan, and go from there.

And while we're at it, don't be afraid to fail. Seriously. Failure isn't the end of the world; it's just a stepping stone. Every time you trip and fall, you learn something new. It's like a toddler learning to walk. They fall a million times, but they keep getting back up until they're running around like crazy. You can do the same!

Now, let's talk about self-care. You can't pour from an empty cup, right? Make sure you're taking care of yourself—physically, mentally, and emotionally. Exercise, eat well, and don't forget to get enough sleep. When you feel good, your mindset naturally shifts to a more positive place.

Let's also touch on mindfulness. Practicing mindfulness can help you stay present and appreciate what you have right now. Whether it's through meditation, yoga, or just taking a moment to breathe deeply, being mindful helps ground you. It pulls you out of that scarcity mindset and reminds you of the abundance that's already in your life.

And remember, it's totally normal to have off days. Some days, you might feel like you're back to square one. That's okay! The key is to be gentle with yourself. Acknowledge where you are, but don't dwell on it. Just like a rubber band, you can stretch and snap back to your positive mindset.

Lastly, don't forget to celebrate your journey. Give yourself a pat on the back for every little win. Whether it's sticking to your new habits for a week or having a great conversation, celebrate it! It reinforces that abundance mindset and keeps you motivated to keep going.

Creating a prosperity mindset isn't just about thinking positively; it's about taking action, surrounding yourself with the right people, and being kind to yourself along the way. It's a journey, and every step you take is a step toward a richer, more fulfilling life.

So, are you ready to dive in? Embrace the challenges, soak up the good vibes, and watch as your life transforms. You've got this! The world is a buffet of opportunities, and it's time to dig in. Grab that fork and get ready to savor every bite!

Chapter 8

The Importance of Setting Goals

Setting goals is like drawing a map for your journey to abundance. It's that simple. When you have clear goals, you're not just wandering around aimlessly; you're headed somewhere with purpose. Think of it this way: without a destination, how can you expect to arrive anywhere? Clarity in your goals creates a beacon of light, guiding you through the fog of uncertainty and doubt. It's your compass, your North Star.

Now, let's dive into how to set those meaningful goals and make 'em stick. First off, you gotta be specific. Vague goals like "I want to be rich" don't cut it. Instead, say, "I want to earn $100,000 a year by starting my own business." See the difference? The first goal is as blurry as a foggy morning, while the second one is as sharp as a tack.

Next, break those big dreams into bite-sized pieces. You wouldn't try to eat a whole pizza in one bite, right? Same goes for your goals. Divide 'em into smaller, manageable tasks. If your big goal is to write a book, start with a chapter outline. Then tackle one chapter at a time. Celebrate each small win—because, trust me, those little victories are what keep the fire burning.

And don't forget about deadlines. Goals without deadlines are just dreams. Set a timeline for each goal. It creates a sense of urgency, pushing you to take action. You might say, "I want to finish my book by the end of the year." Now you've got a timeline to work with, and that'll keep you motivated.

Speaking of motivation, let's chat about the connection between goals and motivation. Goals are like the fuel for your fire. When you set a goal that truly resonates with you, it sparks that inner drive. It's the reason you get up in the morning, the reason you push through the tough days. If your goal feels meaningful, it's gonna light a fire under you.

But what happens when motivation wanes? It's natural, folks. We all have those days when the couch looks more inviting than our to-do list. That's where your why comes into play. Your "why" is the reason behind your goal. Why do you want to achieve this? Is it for financial freedom? To provide for your family? To live a life of adventure? Keep that why front and center. Write it down, stick it on your wall, or make it your screensaver. When the going gets tough, remind yourself why you started in the first place.

Another powerful technique is visualization. Picture yourself achieving your goals. Close your eyes and imagine what it feels like. What does success look like? What are you doing? Who are you with? Visualization is like a mental rehearsal, and it can be a game-changer. The more vividly you can see your success, the more motivated you'll feel to make it a reality.

Now, let's talk about accountability. Sharing your goals with someone you trust can be a huge motivator. Whether it's a friend, family member, or a mentor, having someone to check in with keeps you on track. You're more likely to follow through when someone else is rooting for you. It's like having a cheerleader in your corner, and we all need that extra push sometimes.

And remember, it's okay to adjust your goals along the way. Life's a winding road, and sometimes you gotta take a detour. If something isn't working, don't be afraid to pivot. Your goals should evolve as you grow. It's not about being rigid; it's about being flexible and adapting to the changes life throws at you.

As you embark on this goal-setting journey, embrace the joy of the process. It's not just about the end result; it's about who you become along the way. Each step you take, every challenge you face, it all shapes you into a stronger, more resilient person.

So, let's recap. Clear goals pave the way for abundance by giving you direction and purpose. Use specific, measurable goals and break 'em down into manageable tasks. Set deadlines to create urgency, and always keep your "why" in mind to fuel your motivation. Visualize your success, find an accountability buddy, and don't hesitate to adjust your goals as needed.

Now, take a deep breath and visualize yourself at the finish line. Feel that rush of accomplishment. You've got this! Your journey to abundance is just beginning, and setting those goals is the first step on that exciting path. Keep pushing forward, and remember: every small step is a step toward your dreams. You're not just writing a book or building a business; you're crafting a life filled with purpose and abundance. Now, go out there and make it happen!

Chapter 9

Cultivating a Positive Environment

There's a saying that goes, "You are the average of the five people you spend the most time with." Now, let that sink in for a minute. Your surroundings—the people, the places, the vibes—have a huge impact on your mindset and your journey to abundance. Picture your environment as a garden. If you plant seeds in rocky soil with little sunlight, those seeds are gonna struggle to grow. But if you give them rich soil, plenty of water, and a little sunshine, you'll see them thrive. Your mindset is no different.

First off, let's talk about the impact of your surroundings. You ever walk into a room and just feel the energy? Maybe it's a cozy coffee shop buzzing with laughter, or a cluttered office that feels like a pressure cooker. The energy of your environment can either lift you up or weigh you down. When you're surrounded by positivity, encouragement, and support, it's like having a cheerleading squad for your dreams. But when you're in a negative space, it can feel like you're trying to run a marathon with weights strapped to your back.

So, how do you create that supportive and uplifting space? Start by taking a good, hard look at your environment. What's working? What's not? Is your workspace filled with clutter that distracts you? Or is it a haven of inspiration with quotes that make you smile? Here are some strategies to help you cultivate that positive environment:

1. Declutter and Organize: A tidy space equals a tidy mind. Take some time to clear out

the clutter. Keep only what sparks joy and serves a purpose. You'll be amazed at how a clean space can lift your spirits.

2. Infuse Your Space with Positivity: Surround yourself with things that inspire you. Maybe it's artwork that resonates with your soul, or plants that bring life into your space. Fill your environment with reminders of your goals and dreams.

3. Set Boundaries: Protect your space from negativity. If certain people drain your energy or bring you down, it's okay to create some distance. Your mental well-being is worth it.

4. Create Rituals: Establish daily rituals that ground you. Whether it's a morning coffee on your porch or a quiet moment of reflection, these rituals can help you center yourself and set a positive tone for the day.

5. Embrace Nature: Don't underestimate the power of the great outdoors. Spend time in nature, breathe in the fresh air, and let the beauty of the world around you fill you with peace and abundance.

Now, let's dive into the role of community in fostering abundance. We are social creatures, folks. We thrive on connection. Think about it—when you're part of a community that uplifts and supports you, it's like having a safety net. You're not just chasing your dreams alone; you've got a whole crew cheering you on.

Here's the deal: find your tribe. Seek out people who inspire you, challenge you, and share your values. Whether it's a book club, a networking group, or just a circle of friends who get you, these connections can make all the difference. Here are some ways to cultivate a supportive community:

1. Attend Workshops and Events: Look for workshops, seminars, or local meetups that align with your interests. You never know who you'll meet or what inspiration you'll find.

2. Be Vulnerable: Don't be afraid to share your struggles and triumphs with others. Vulnerability fosters connection. You'll find that others resonate with your journey, and together, you can lift each other up.

3. Offer Support: Be the kind of friend you want to have. Offer your support and encouragement to others. When you give, you receive, and that creates a beautiful cycle of abundance.

4. Collaborate: Seek out opportunities to collaborate with others. Whether it's a joint project, a co-hosted event, or simply

brainstorming ideas together, collaboration can lead to incredible growth.

5. Celebrate Each Other: Take the time to celebrate the wins, big and small. A simple "I'm proud of you" can go a long way in building a positive community.

As you cultivate your positive environment and surround yourself with uplifting people, remember that abundance is not just about material wealth. It's about the richness of experiences, connections, and the joy of living fully. When you create a space that nurtures your spirit and fosters community, you're opening the door to a world of possibilities.

So, take a moment to visualize your ideal environment. What does it look like? How does it feel? Picture yourself thriving in that space, surrounded by supportive people who believe in you. Let that vision guide you as you take steps to create your own garden of abundance.

You've got the power to shape your environment and cultivate the mindset you desire. Embrace it. You're not just a passive observer in your life; you're the gardener, planting seeds of positivity and watching them bloom. Keep nurturing that space, and watch as abundance flows into your life in ways you never thought possible.

Now, go out there and start making those changes. You've got this! Your journey to abundance is just beginning, and the world is waiting for you to shine.

Chapter 10

Mindfulness and Presence

Let's get one thing straight: mindfulness isn't just some trendy buzzword that folks toss around to sound enlightened. Nah, it's way more than that. Think of mindfulness as a powerful tool—like a secret key that unlocks the door to a treasure trove of abundance. Imagine it's a pair of glasses that lets you see all the riches surrounding you, riches you might miss in the daily grind. When you practice mindfulness, you're not just daydreaming; you're sharpening your awareness and tuning into the beauty of the present moment.

Picture this: you're strolling down a street you've walked a million times, lost in thought about that never-ending to-do list or that project looming at work. Then, bam! You spot a vibrant flower blooming by the sidewalk. That moment? Pure magic. The color pops, the fragrance hits you, and suddenly you're hit with a wave of joy and gratitude. That's mindfulness doing its thing. It pulls you back into the now, reminding you that life's full of gifts—big and small. By embracing mindfulness, you shift your focus from what you lack to what you already have.

Now, let's dive into how to sprinkle mindfulness into your everyday life. Spoiler alert: it doesn't have to be a complicated process or a time-sucker. Start small. Maybe kick off your day with a few minutes of mindful breathing. Find a comfy spot, close your eyes, and take a deep breath in through your nose. Let that belly of yours expand like a balloon. Hold it for a sec, then exhale slowly through your mouth. While you're breathing, focus on how the air fills your lungs and how it feels to let it all go. Just five minutes of this can ground you and set a positive tone for your day.

And hey, let's talk about mindful eating. Next time you sit down for a meal, take a moment to appreciate the colors, textures, and aromas of your food. Don't just shovel it in—chew slowly, savoring each bite. Notice how the flavors unfold like a story on your palate. This isn't just about enjoying your food; it's about building a deeper connection to the present moment and recognizing the nourishment you're receiving. You might be surprised at how this practice can totally change your relationship with food and boost your overall sense of abundance.

Mindfulness can even sneak into those mundane tasks we all have to do. Washing dishes? Foldin' laundry? Going for a walk? Try to engage fully with the experience. Feel the warmth of the water on your hands, the texture of the fabric, or the rhythm of your footsteps. By immersing yourself in these moments, you create a sense of presence that enriches your daily life.

Let's chat about the connection between presence and prosperity. When you're fully present, you're like a radar picking up on opportunities zipping your way. You might notice a chance encounter with someone who could be a valuable connection or an idea that sparks a new venture. But when your mind's cluttered with worries about tomorrow or regrets about yesterday, you might miss those golden moments. And who wants to do that?

Being present also cranks up your gratitude levels. When you're grounded in the now, you can appreciate the little things—the laughter of a friend, the warmth of the sun on your skin, or the cozy comfort of your home. This gratitude shifts your energy, attracting more positive experiences into your life. It's a beautiful cycle: the more you appreciate what you have, the more you open yourself up to receiving even more.

Think of presence as a magnet for prosperity. When you're focused on the here and now, you're sending a message to the universe that you're ready to receive. You're basically saying, "Hey, I see the abundance around me, and I'm open to more." This openness creates a flow of energy that invites opportunities, resources, and relationships that align with your desires.

So, how do you cultivate this presence? One effective way is through meditation. Don't sweat it; it doesn't have to be a long, drawn-out process. Even just a few minutes a day can make a world of difference. Find a quiet space, sit comfortably, and focus on your breath. If your mind wanders—and trust me, it will—gently bring your attention back to your breath. This practice trains your mind to stay present, and over time, you'll find it easier to carry that presence into your daily life.

Another approach? Create mindful moments throughout your day. Set a timer for a few minutes and pick an activity to do mindfully. It could be sipping your morning coffee, listening to music, or even taking a shower. Focus entirely on the sensations, sounds, and feelings of that moment. This simple practice can help anchor you in the present and cultivate a sense of abundance.

And here's the kicker: mindfulness is a journey, not a destination. It's all about progress, not perfection. Celebrate those small wins along the way. Each time you catch yourself being present, give yourself a mental high-five. You're building a new habit, one that'll enrich your life and deepen your sense of abundance.

Incorporating mindfulness into your life isn't just about sharpening your awareness; it's about transforming your relationship with abundance. As you become more mindful, you'll start to notice how prosperity flows into your life. You'll see the universe is generous, providing you with opportunities, resources, and connections that align with your goals. The more you practice being present, the more you'll recognize the abundance that's already yours.

Now, let's be real. It's not always easy to stay mindful. Life throws curveballs, distractions pop up, and sometimes you just wanna zone out. But that's okay! It's part of the process. The key is to be gentle with yourself. When you slip up, just acknowledge it and refocus. You're not aiming for perfection; you're aiming for progress.

Speaking of distractions, ever notice how easy it is to get lost in your phone? Social media, endless scrolling, notifications pinging—it's like a black hole for your attention. Instead of mindlessly scrolling, try taking a mindful break. Put your phone down, take a deep breath, and observe your surroundings. What do you see? What do you hear? What do you feel? It's a quick way to pull yourself back into the present and shake off that digital fog.

Let's not forget about gratitude journaling. It's a simple yet powerful practice. Grab a notebook and jot down a few things you're grateful for each day. They can be big or small—maybe it's a delicious cup of coffee, a chat with a friend, or even just the sunshine peeking through your window. This practice helps shift your focus to the positive aspects of your life, reinforcing that sense of abundance.

And hey, have you ever tried mindful walking? It's like a moving meditation. Instead of rushing from point A to point B, slow down. Pay attention to each step. Feel the ground beneath your feet, notice the rhythm of your breath, and take in the sights and sounds around you. You'll be amazed at how much more you notice when you're fully present in the moment.

Now, let's talk about the power of community. Surrounding yourself with like-minded folks can amplify your mindfulness journey. Join a local meditation group, attend workshops, or even just chat with friends about mindfulness. Sharing experiences and insights can deepen your understanding and keep you motivated. Plus, it's always nice to have a support system when you're trying to make changes in your life.

But remember, mindfulness isn't a one-size-fits-all approach. What works for one person might not work for you, and that's totally cool. Experiment with different practices and find what resonates with you. Whether it's meditation, yoga, or just taking a few moments to breathe, the important thing is to find what helps you connect with the present moment.

Now, I've gotta throw in a little humor here. Sometimes, we can take mindfulness too seriously. Like, we think we have to be perfect at it, or that we need to meditate for hours on end. But let's be real—life's messy! Embrace the chaos. Laugh at the little things. If you find yourself getting frustrated, take a step back and chuckle. After all, mindfulness is about being present, not about being perfect.

So, as you move forward, embrace mindfulness with open arms. Allow it to guide you on your journey to prosperity and peace. You've got this! With each mindful moment, you're not just enhancing your awareness of abundance; you're stepping into a life filled with possibility and joy. Your path to unlimited abundance is waiting, and it starts right here, right now. Let's dive in and make the most of it!

And remember, mindfulness is a practice, not a performance. There's no scoreboard, no judges, and no right or wrong way to do it. It's all about finding what feels good for you and allowing yourself to be present in each moment. So go ahead, take a deep breath, and embrace the beautiful mess that is life. You're doing great, and every little step counts. Let's keep this journey going!

Chapter 11

Embracing Change and Growth

Change is as certain as the sunrise. It's the very heartbeat of life, a rhythm that propels us toward abundance. Now, I know what you might be thinkin'—change can feel downright scary. It can shake us to our core, make us question everything we thought we knew. But let me tell you, my friend, it's also the gateway to everything you desire. To unlock that unlimited abundance, you gotta embrace change with open arms.

Think about it. When a seed is planted, it doesn't just sit there, comfortable in the soil. No, it stretches and pushes through, breaking free to reach for the sun. That's change, my friend! It's necessary for growth. Without it, we'd stay stuck in the same old patterns, never discovering the wealth of opportunities waiting just beyond our comfort zone. So, let's dive into understanding how to navigate this change gracefully and cultivate a growth mindset that'll help you achieve your goals.

First off, let's get real about change. It's not just about the big stuff—losing a job, moving to a new city, or starting a family. Change happens in the little moments too. It's that feeling when you decide to try a new approach to a problem, or when you choose to let go of a limiting belief that's been holding you back. Each time you embrace change, you're taking a step toward abundance.

Now, how do you navigate this change without losing your mind? Here are some strategies to help you glide through life's transitions with grace:

1. **Stay Present**: The future can be a daunting place if you let your mind run wild. Focus on the here and now. Take a deep breath, and remind yourself that you have the tools to handle whatever comes your way.

2. **Reframe Your Perspective**: Instead of seeing change as a threat, view it as an opportunity. What can you learn from this situation? How can it help you grow? Flip that script and watch how your mindset shifts.

3. **Seek Support**: You don't have to go through change alone. Reach out to friends, family, or mentors who can provide guidance and encouragement. Sometimes, just hearing

someone say, "You got this!" can make all the difference.

4. **Practice Self-Compassion**: Change can be tough, and it's okay to feel overwhelmed. Be kind to yourself. Recognize that it's perfectly normal to struggle during transitions. Allow yourself to feel those emotions without judgment.

5. **Celebrate Small Wins**: Each step you take toward embracing change is a victory. Whether it's making a tough decision or simply getting through a challenging day, take a moment to acknowledge your progress.

Now, let's talk about the growth mindset. This isn't just some fancy buzzword; it's a powerful tool that can transform your life. A growth mindset means you believe your abilities and intelligence can be developed with effort and perseverance. It's about seeing challenges as stepping stones rather than roadblocks.

Here's why a growth mindset is crucial for achieving your goals:

- **Resilience**: When you encounter setbacks, a growth mindset helps you bounce back. Instead of throwing in the towel, you'll see these challenges as opportunities to learn and improve.

- **Increased Motivation**: With a growth mindset, you're more likely to push yourself to take risks and try new things. You'll feel energized by the prospect of growth, and that motivation will fuel your journey toward abundance.

- **Enhanced Creativity**: Embracing change opens the door to new ideas and solutions. When you're willing to think outside the box, you'll discover innovative ways to overcome obstacles and achieve your goals.

- **Stronger Relationships**: A growth mindset fosters collaboration and support. When you believe in growth, you're more likely to uplift others and seek out connections that encourage mutual development.

To cultivate this mindset, consider these practical exercises:

1. **Embrace Challenges**: Seek out tasks that push you beyond your comfort zone. Whether it's taking a class, starting a new project, or having a difficult conversation, embrace the discomfort.

2. **Reflect on Failures**: Instead of shying away from failure, analyze what went wrong and how you can improve next time. Each failure is a lesson in disguise, waiting to propel you forward.

3. **Surround Yourself with Growth-Oriented People**: Find a community of like-minded individuals who value growth and positivity. Their energy will inspire you to keep moving forward.

4. **Keep a Journal**: Document your journey. Write about your experiences with change, your goals, and your reflections on growth. This practice will help you track your progress and celebrate your achievements.

5. **Visualize Your Success**: Picture yourself thriving amidst change. What does that look like? How does it feel? Visualization can

be a powerful motivator, helping you stay focused on your goals.

As you embrace change and nurture a growth mindset, remember that this journey isn't just about you. The impact of your growth extends far beyond your own life. By stepping into your abundance, you inspire others to do the same. You become a beacon of hope and possibility, lighting the way for those around you.

So, my friend, as you navigate the waves of change, keep your eyes on the horizon. Visualize the abundant life you're creating, and trust that every step you take is leading you closer to your dreams. Embrace the lessons, celebrate the growth, and know that you are more capable than you can imagine.

Now, go on and take that leap. The world is waiting for you to unlock your unlimited abundance. You got this!

Chapter 12

Building Healthy Financial Habits

Let's dive into the world of money, shall we? Yeah, I get it—talking about finances can feel like a drag sometimes. But hang tight, 'cause we're about to kickstart some healthy financial habits that'll set you up for a lifetime of chill vibes and cash flow. Think of budgeting as your trusty roadmap. It's not just about counting coins; it's about steering your financial ship in the right direction. Seriously, you wouldn't hit the open sea without a map, right? So why would you navigate your finances without a solid budget?

Picture a budget as your compass. It helps you see where your money's flowing. It's a handy tool that gives you the full picture. You can track your income, your expenses, and—here's the kicker—spot areas where you can stash some cash. It's all about making informed choices. When you know where every dollar is going, you can make decisions that align with your goals. Want to save for that dream vacation? Or maybe you've got your eye on a cozy little home of your own? A budget helps you carve out that path.

Now, let's be real—budgeting doesn't have to be a snooze fest. Make it fun! Use apps, spreadsheets, or even good ol' pen and paper. Find a method that clicks with you. And hey, it's not set in stone. Life throws curveballs, and so can your budget. Be flexible, adjust when necessary, and keep your eyes on the prize.

But hold up, we're just getting started. Saving and investing wisely are the next big steps on this journey. Think of saving like planting seeds. You nurture them, water them, and with time, they grow. Start small if you need to—set aside a little each month. You'd be amazed at how fast those savings can pile up. And when you're ready, consider investing. It's like putting your money to work for you. Whether it's stocks, bonds, or mutual funds, the key is to educate yourself first.

Now, I can almost hear you thinking, "But I don't know anything about investing!" Chill out! Financial literacy is your best buddy. It's the knowledge that empowers you to make smart decisions. Start reading books, listening to podcasts, or attending workshops. Get curious! The more you learn, the more confident you'll feel about your financial choices.

And let's not forget, financial literacy isn't just about crunching numbers. It's about recognizing your worth and believing you can create a life of abundance. When you get the hang of managing your money, you're taking control. You're saying, "I got this!" And that mindset? It's everything.

Here's a little exercise for you. Grab a notebook and jot down your financial goals. Maybe it's paying off debt, saving for retirement, or just having a little cushion for emergencies. Write 'em down, and then break them into smaller, actionable steps. This way, you're not overwhelmed; you're empowered.

Next up, let's chat about the beauty of automation. Set up automatic transfers to your savings or investment accounts. It's like putting your finances on autopilot. You won't even notice the money's gone, and before you know it, you'll have built a nice little nest egg. It's all about making those healthy habits stick.

As you embark on this journey, remember to celebrate your wins—no matter how small. Did you stick to your budget this month? High five! Did you save a little extra? Do a little happy dance! These small victories will keep you motivated and remind you that you're making progress.

Now, let's wrap this up with a little reminder: building healthy financial habits is a marathon, not a sprint. It takes time, patience, and a whole lot of perseverance. But you can do this. You have the power to create a life filled with abundance and peace. Embrace the journey, learn as you go, and keep your eyes on that horizon. Your financial future is bright, my friend!

But wait, there's more! Let's dig deeper into some practical tips that can help you build those financial habits. I mean, who doesn't want to be financially savvy, right?

First things first—let's talk about the importance of tracking your expenses. You've gotta know where your money is going if you want to take charge. It's like that classic saying, "Out of sight, out of mind." If you don't keep tabs on your spending, you might find yourself in a pickle. So, grab that budgeting app or a simple spreadsheet, and start logging every dollar you spend. Yeah, it might feel tedious at first, but trust me, it'll pay off in the long run.

You might find it eye-opening to see where you're blowing your cash. Maybe you're spending way too much on takeout or those fancy coffee runs. I mean, we all love a good latte, but is it worth sacrificing your savings for? Keep it real. Once you identify those sneaky expenses, you can make adjustments. Maybe you cut back on the takeout and whip up some meals at home. It's healthier for your wallet and your waistline!

Now, let's get into the nitty-gritty of setting up an emergency fund. Life's unpredictable, and you never know when you might need a little financial cushion. Whether it's a surprise car repair or an unexpected medical bill, having that safety net can save you from a world of stress. Aim to save at least three to six months' worth of living expenses. It sounds like a lot, but take it one step at a time. Start small, and build it up gradually.

And hey, let's not forget about debt. If you've got any lingering debt, tackling it should be a priority. It's like that annoying itch you can't scratch. The sooner you deal with it, the better you'll feel. Consider the snowball method—pay off your smallest debts first, then move on to the bigger ones. It's all about gaining momentum and feeling that sweet satisfaction of knocking out those balances.

Speaking of satisfaction, let's chat about the power of rewards. You've been working hard on your financial habits, so why not treat yourself once in a while? Set up some milestones—maybe when you hit a certain savings goal or pay off a debt. Celebrate those wins! It doesn't have to be anything extravagant; even a nice dinner out or a new book can do the trick. Just don't go overboard and blow your budget in the process.

Now, let's touch on the importance of financial goals. We've mentioned them before, but let's break it down a bit more. Setting clear, achievable goals gives you something to strive for. It's like having a finish line in a race. You wouldn't run a marathon without knowing where the finish line is, right? So, whether it's saving for a vacation, a new car, or your dream home, write those goals down and keep them visible.

And while we're at it, don't forget to revisit those goals regularly. Life changes, and so should your financial plans. Maybe you get a promotion, or perhaps you decide to start a family. Whatever the case, check in on your goals and adjust as needed.

Let's also chat about the importance of surrounding yourself with the right people. Ever heard the saying, "You are the average of the five people you spend the most time with"? Well, it rings true. If you hang out with folks who are financially savvy, chances are you'll pick up some good habits. Share your goals with them, ask for advice, and celebrate each other's wins. It's all about building a support system.

Now, let's get a little personal. Think about your own relationship with money. How did your upbringing shape your views? Did your parents talk openly about finances, or was it a taboo subject? Understanding your money mindset can help you break free from any limiting beliefs. Maybe you grew up thinking money is scarce, or perhaps you believe it's a tool for freedom. Whatever it is, take a moment to reflect on it.

And let's be real—money isn't everything. It's a tool, sure, but it's not the end-all-be-all. What truly matters is how you use it to create the life you want. It's about experiences, relationships, and finding joy in the little things. So, as you build those financial habits, keep that perspective in mind.

Now, let's get back to the nitty-gritty. Have you ever thought about diversifying your income? Relying on a single source can be risky. Think about ways to earn extra cash on the side. Maybe it's freelancing, starting a small business, or even picking up a part-time gig. It doesn't have to be a huge commitment; just something to boost your income and give you a little cushion.

And while we're at it, let's chat about the importance of retirement planning. I know, I know—it feels like a million years away. But trust me, the earlier you start, the better off you'll be. Take advantage of employer-sponsored retirement plans, like a 401(k). If they match your contributions, that's free money! It's like finding cash in your coat pocket.

But wait, there's more! Look into IRAs (Individual Retirement Accounts) too. They're a great way to save for retirement with some tax benefits. The key is to start early and let that money grow over time. Compound interest is your friend—trust me on this one.

As we wrap things up, let's revisit that idea of celebrating your wins. You've been on this journey, building healthy financial habits, and you deserve to acknowledge your progress. Maybe you set a goal to save a certain amount this month, and you crushed it! Throw a mini celebration. Treat yourself to a nice dinner, or take a day off to do something you love.

And remember, it's all about the journey. Building healthy financial habits is a process, and it won't happen overnight. Be patient with yourself. There'll be ups and downs along the way, but that's all part of the ride. Keep learning, keep growing, and keep pushing towards those goals.

So, what's the takeaway here? Money management isn't just about crunching numbers; it's about creating a life you love. It's about making choices that align with your values and dreams. You've got the power to shape your financial future, so embrace it!

In the end, it's about living life on your terms. Whether that means traveling the world, buying your dream home, or simply enjoying a stress-free life, you've got what it takes. So go out there, build those healthy financial habits, and make your dreams a reality. Your financial future is bright, my friend!

And who knows? Maybe one day you'll look back on this journey and be proud of how far you've come. You'll be living proof that with a little effort, a sprinkle of patience, and a whole lot of determination, you can create the life you've always wanted. Now, get out there and start making those financial habits stick!

Chapter 13

The Role of Giving and Generosity

You know, there's something magical about giving. It's like flipping a switch that lights up your heart and soul. When you give, whether it's your time, resources, or love, you start to feel this swell of abundance within you. It's as if you're saying to the universe, "Hey, I'm open for business! Bring it on!" And guess what? The universe listens.

Think about it for a second. When you give, you're not just handing over something; you're creating a ripple effect. Imagine tossing a pebble into a still pond. The ripples spread out, touching everything in their path. That's exactly what generosity does. It touches lives, creates connections, and, believe it or not, it can even enhance your own prosperity.

Now, let's break it down a bit. When you give, you're actively engaging in a mindset of abundance. You're saying, "I have enough to share." This simple shift in perspective can change your entire outlook on life. It's like putting on a pair of glasses that lets you see the world in vibrant colors instead of dull grays.

And here's the kicker: when you give, you often find that your own needs are met in unexpected ways. Maybe you donate your time to a local charity, and in return, you meet someone who offers you a job opportunity. Or perhaps you lend a hand to a friend, and they end up introducing you to a network that opens doors you never knew existed.

Now, let's talk about practical ways to weave giving into your everyday life. It doesn't have to be grand gestures or big-ticket items. Start small. Hold the door open for someone, offer a compliment, or share a meal with someone in need. Each act of kindness is a seed planted in the garden of abundance.

You could also consider volunteering your time. Find a cause that resonates with you— maybe it's mentoring young people, helping out at an animal shelter, or participating in community clean-ups. The time you invest in others will come back to you tenfold, filling your life with purpose and connection.

Another beautiful way to give is through your skills. Are you a whiz at graphic design? Offer to create a logo for a small business. Can you bake a mean pie? Share some with your neighbors or a local shelter. Your talents are gifts, and sharing them can create a profound impact.

Let's not forget about the power of listening. Sometimes, all someone needs is a compassionate ear. When you take the time to truly listen to someone, you're giving them a gift that can't be wrapped up in a box. You're validating their feelings and experiences, and that's a priceless treasure.

As you incorporate giving into your life, remember to keep your heart open. It's not about expecting something in return; it's about embracing the joy that comes from selflessness. When you give freely, you create a cycle of generosity that flows back to you in ways you might never have imagined.

So, let's wrap this up with a little challenge. I want you to commit to one act of giving this week. It could be as simple as sending a heartfelt note to a friend or as involved as organizing a community event. Whatever it is, make it meaningful to you.

As you step into this journey of giving, visualize the abundance it brings. Picture the connections you'll make, the joy you'll spread, and the prosperity that will flow into your life. You've got this! Remember, every little bit counts. Each act of kindness is a building block in the foundation of your abundant life.

Now go on, unleash your generous spirit, and watch how the universe responds! You're not just changing the world around you; you're transforming your own life in the process. Embrace the power of giving, and let it lead you to a life filled with prosperity and peace.

Chapter 14

Nurturing Relationships for Success

Life's a wild ride, isn't it? And if you think about it, relationships are like the threads weaving through this chaotic tapestry. They're what keep everything from unraveling. Your personal growth, your finances, your happiness—they're all tangled up in the connections you make. Those bonds can either lift you to the skies or drag you down into the mud. It's like having a solid bridge over raging waters or a flimsy old plank that's just begging to snap. So, when you put in the work to nurture supportive relationships, you're not just doing it for others; you're doing it for yourself, too.

Let's get real for a sec. Relationships are golden keys to doors you didn't even know existed. Picture this: you're at a networking shindig, and you start chatting with someone who's just as fired up about entrepreneurship as you are. That casual convo could turn into a partnership that sends your business into the stratosphere. Or maybe you stumble upon a mentor who helps you dodge the financial landmines. These connections? They're like hidden treasures waiting for you to dig 'em up.

But hold up! It's not all roses and sunshine. Building and keeping these connections takes some serious hustle. Think of it like gardening; you can't just toss some seeds in the dirt and hope for the best. You gotta water it, yank out the weeds, and sometimes trim it back to help it thrive. So, here are some solid strategies to help you grow those supportive relationships:

First off, be genuine. Authenticity is like a magnet. People can sniff out fake vibes from a mile away. When you come at relationships with honesty and a bit of vulnerability, you create a safe space for others to do the same. Share your dreams, fears, and stories. You'd be amazed at how much deeper your connections can get when you open up.

Next up, listen actively. Seriously, this one's a game changer! When someone's talking, really tune in. Ditch your phone, make eye contact, and show you care. Active listening not only strengthens your bond but also opens up paths for collaboration. You never know what nuggets of wisdom or opportunities might pop up from a heartfelt chat.

And don't forget to show appreciation. A little gratitude can go a long way. A simple "thank you" or a heartfelt note can brighten someone's day and reinforce your connection.

Celebrate their wins, too! When you lift others up, it creates a ripple effect that often comes back around to you.

Be supportive. Life's a rollercoaster ride, and we all hit those ups and downs. Be the person who's there to cheer on your friends and family during their victories and comfort them when things get tough. Your support can be a lifeline, and it strengthens those bonds you share.

Collaboration is where the magic happens! Working together towards a common goal can deepen your relationships and lead to incredible outcomes. Whether it's a joint project, a community service gig, or just brainstorming ideas, collaboration fosters a sense of unity and purpose.

Now, let's dive into why collaboration is key to achieving abundance. It's pretty simple—two (or more) heads are better than one. When you team up, you're mixing strengths, ideas, and resources. It's like blending paint; the result can be a vibrant masterpiece that none of you could've whipped up alone.

Think about those successful partnerships in business or life. They often grow from a foundation of trust and mutual respect. When you collaborate, you're not just pooling resources; you're also expanding your network. Each person brings their own circle of influence, opening up even more doors.

And here's the kicker—collaboration can spark creativity. Surround yourself with diverse perspectives, and you'll be more likely to think outside the box. New ideas thrive in an environment where collaboration is encouraged.

So don't shy away from teaming up with others. Embrace it!

While you're nurturing relationships for success, remember it's not just about what you can snag; it's also about what you can give. Be the person who lifts others up, and you'll find that abundance flows back to you in ways you never expected. It's like planting seeds of kindness that bloom into a garden of opportunities.

As you embark on this journey of nurturing relationships, keep in mind that it's a continuous process. Just like any living thing, relationships need care and attention. So, make it a priority to check in with your connections regularly. A quick message or a coffee catch-up can do wonders for strengthening your bond.

Visualize your success not just in terms of personal achievements but in the connections you build along the way. Imagine the joy of celebrating milestones with those who've had your back through thick and thin. Picture yourself collaborating with like-minded folks who inspire you to reach new heights. That's the beauty of nurturing relationships for success.

So, roll up your sleeves, get out there, and start cultivating those connections. You've got this! The world is packed with potential allies waiting to join you on your journey. Embrace the power of relationships, and watch as your personal and financial growth flourishes like a well-tended garden.

At the end of the day, it all boils down to this: relationships are the heartbeat of abundance. Nurture them, cherish them, and let them guide you toward a life filled with prosperity and peace. Your journey is just getting started, and the connections you make along the way will be the wind beneath your wings. So spread those wings wide, my friend, and soar!

Now, let's dive a little deeper. Think about the folks you've connected with over the years. Who's been a game changer for you? Maybe it's that one friend who always pushes you to chase your dreams or that mentor who took you under their wing. These relationships don't just pop up overnight. They take time, effort, and a sprinkle of vulnerability.

Take a moment to reflect on how you nurture these connections. Are you reaching out enough? Are you genuinely interested in their lives? It's easy to get caught up in our own hustle and forget about the people who matter. But remember, it's a two-way street. You gotta give to get.

Let's chat about the power of vulnerability for a sec. It's not always easy to open up, but it can be a game changer. When you share your struggles or fears, it encourages others to do the same. It creates a bond that's built on trust and understanding. Think about it—when was the last time you had a deep conversation that left you feeling connected? That's the magic of vulnerability.

And hey, don't underestimate the power of a simple check-in. Life gets busy, and sometimes we forget to reach out. A quick text or a coffee date can mean the world to someone. It shows you care, and it keeps the connection alive. Plus, you never know what you might learn from that chat.

Now, let's talk about setting boundaries. Yeah, it sounds a bit counterintuitive when we're talking about nurturing relationships, but hear me out. Healthy boundaries are crucial.

They protect your energy and ensure that your relationships are balanced. It's okay to say no sometimes. It doesn't make you a bad friend; it makes you a smart one.

Think about it this way: if you're constantly giving and never receiving, you'll burn out. And that's not good for anyone. So, be mindful of your limits. Communicate them clearly, and you'll find that your relationships become stronger and more fulfilling.

And while we're on the subject of boundaries, let's not forget about the importance of surrounding yourself with the right people. You know the saying, "You are the average of the five people you spend the most time with"? It's true! Choose your crew wisely. Surround yourself with folks who inspire you, challenge you, and lift you up.

But what if you find yourself in a toxic relationship? That's a tough spot to be in. Sometimes, it's best to cut ties. It's not easy, but your mental health matters. You can't thrive if you're constantly dragging around negativity. Trust your gut, and don't be afraid to make the tough calls.

Now, let's get back to collaboration. It's such a powerful tool for success. Think about the last time you worked with someone on a project. Wasn't it refreshing to bounce ideas off each other? To see things from a different perspective? That's the beauty of collaboration. It's not just about getting things done; it's about the journey and the relationships you build along the way.

And speaking of collaboration, don't be afraid to seek out diverse perspectives. We all come from different backgrounds and experiences, and that's what makes teamwork so rich. Embrace the differences. They can lead to innovative solutions and creative breakthroughs.

Let's not forget about the role of technology in nurturing relationships. We live in a digital age, and while face-to-face interactions are irreplaceable, online connections can be just as valuable. Social media, video calls, and messaging apps can help you stay in touch with people who matter, no matter the distance. Just remember to keep it real. Don't let the digital world replace genuine connections.

As you move forward, keep an eye out for opportunities to give back. Whether it's mentoring someone, volunteering, or simply being there for a friend in need, giving back strengthens your relationships. It creates a sense of community and belonging. Plus, it feels good to know you're making a difference.

And hey, don't forget to celebrate the little wins along the way. Every step you take in nurturing your relationships is a step toward success. So, whether it's a heartfelt conversation, a successful collaboration, or simply being there for someone, take a moment to acknowledge it. Celebrate your progress!

Now, let's wrap this up. Nurturing relationships isn't just a nice-to-have; it's a must-have for success. It's about building a network of support, inspiration, and collaboration. It's about lifting each other up and creating a community that thrives together.

So, as you set out on this journey, remember: it's all about connection. It's about nurturing those bonds and watching them grow. You've got the tools, the strategies, and the heart to make it happen. Embrace the journey, and let your relationships guide you to a life filled with abundance and joy.

Now go out there and spread those wings! You're ready to soar!

Chapter 15

Celebrating Your Journey

Life's a wild ride, right? Like a road trip with all the bumps and unexpected turns. And let's be real—if you don't take a sec to soak it all in, you might miss out on some seriously stunning views. Celebrating your journey is like pulling over to take a selfie at a killer overlook. It's about recognizing how far you've come and the progress you've made. So, let's dig into why celebrating your journey is super important, yeah?

First off, let's chat about recognizing your progress. It's all too easy to get swept up in the daily grind, always hustling for that next big thing. But here's the scoop: every little step counts. Whether you just nailed a big goal or just survived a rough day, giving yourself a pat on the back for those moments is crucial. It's not just about the big wins; it's the tiny victories that build you up and keep your fire lit.

Picture this: you're scaling a mountain. You can't see the top from where you're at, but every few steps, you spot a gorgeous flower or a breathtaking view. Those little moments? They remind you that the climb is worth it. When you take a beat to acknowledge your achievements—no matter how small—you're basically saying, "Hey, I'm making progress!" And that's pretty darn empowering.

Now, let's get down to brass tacks. How do you actually reflect on your growth and successes? One killer method is to keep a journal. Seriously, grab a notebook or even your phone and start jotting down your thoughts. At the end of each week, write down three things you accomplished. They can be as simple as finishing a book, having a deep convo, or sticking to your budget. This little exercise doesn't just highlight your progress; it creates a record of your journey that you can look back on.

Another fun idea? Create a "celebration jar." Just find any old jar lying around and fill it with notes about your achievements. Every time you hit a goal or experience a win, write it down on a slip of paper and toss it in. When you're feeling down or need a boost, pull out a few notes and remind yourself of how far you've come. It's like having your own personal cheer squad right there in your living room!

Now, let's talk about the power of celebrating those small wins. It's like tossing fuel on your fire. Each time you acknowledge a success—no matter how tiny—you're building momentum. Think of it like a snowball rolling down a hill. It starts small, but as it picks up more snow, it grows and grows. The more you celebrate, the more fired up you get to tackle the next challenge.

So, how often do you reward yourself? Maybe you treat yourself to your favorite coffee after a productive day or take a moment to enjoy a sunset after a tough week. These little celebrations create a positive feedback loop, encouraging you to keep pushing forward. When you celebrate, you're telling your brain, "This is awesome! Let's do more of this!" And trust me, your brain's paying attention.

But here's the kicker—celebrating isn't just about you. It's also about inspiring others.

When you share your achievements with friends or family, you create a ripple effect. You might just spark someone else's motivation to chase their own dreams. So don't hold back! Share your wins, no matter how small. Celebrate with your loved ones, and watch how it lifts everyone's spirits.

As we wrap this up, keep in mind that your journey is one-of-a-kind, and every step matters. Recognizing your progress and achievements isn't just a nice thought—it's essential for growth. Reflecting on your successes keeps you grounded and connected to your purpose. And celebrating those small wins? That's the fuel that'll keep your fire burning bright.

So go on, take a moment today to celebrate. Whether it's a dance party in your living room or a quiet moment of gratitude, honor your journey. You're doing amazing things, and you deserve to recognize that. Keep climbing, keep celebrating, and watch as abundance flows into your life like a river after a rainstorm. You've got this!

Now, let's dive a little deeper into the nitty-gritty of this whole celebration thing. You might be wondering why it's so important to celebrate in the first place. Well, let's break it down.

When you celebrate, you're not just giving yourself a high-five; you're reinforcing positive behavior. It's like training a puppy—reward them when they do something good, and they're more likely to do it again. The same goes for us humans. Acknowledging your wins, big or small, tells your brain that you're on the right track. It's like a little nudge saying, "Keep going, you're doing great!"

Plus, celebrating helps you build a positive mindset. Life can throw some serious curveballs, and it's easy to get bogged down by negativity. But when you take the time to celebrate, you're shifting your focus from what's going wrong to what's going right. It's like putting on a pair of rose-colored glasses and seeing the world in a whole new light.

And let's not forget about the social aspect of celebration. Humans are social creatures, and sharing your successes with others can create a sense of community. When you celebrate with friends or family, you're not just boosting your own spirits; you're lifting theirs too. It's a win-win situation. Everyone feels good, and you all get to bask in the glow of each other's achievements.

Now, I get it—some folks might feel a bit awkward about celebrating themselves. Maybe you think it's bragging or that you don't deserve it. But let me tell you, that's a load of nonsense. Celebrating your journey isn't about showing off; it's about honoring your hard work and dedication. You've put in the effort, so why not take a moment to recognize that?

Think of it this way: if you don't celebrate your own achievements, who will? It's like throwing a birthday party for someone else but forgetting to celebrate your own special day. You deserve to feel proud of what you've accomplished. So shake off that self-doubt and embrace the joy of celebrating!

Now, let's explore some fun ways to celebrate that you might not have thought of. Sure, there's the classic cake and balloons, but let's get creative!

How about planning a mini-adventure? Treat yourself to a day out exploring somewhere new. Hit up a local museum, take a hike, or visit a nearby town you've never been to. It's all about making memories and treating yourself for the hard work you've put in.

Or maybe you could throw a little gathering with your friends. Invite them over for a potluck, where everyone brings a dish to share. While you're munching on delicious food, take turns sharing your recent wins. It's a great way to bond and uplift each other.

Another idea? Create a vision board! Grab some magazines, scissors, and glue, and start cutting out images and words that inspire you. As you create your board, reflect on your achievements and what you want to celebrate moving forward. It's a fun, creative way to visualize your journey and set new goals.

And let's not forget about self-care. Treat yourself to a spa day at home. Light some candles, run a bubble bath, and indulge in your favorite skincare routine. This isn't just pampering; it's a way to honor yourself and all the hard work you've put in.

But hey, it's not just about the big celebrations. Don't underestimate the power of everyday moments. Celebrate the little things— like finishing a book, getting through a tough week, or even just making it to Friday. Those small moments add up, and they deserve recognition too.

As you go about your day, try to find joy in the little victories. Maybe you cooked a great meal or finally organized that messy closet. Give yourself a mental high-five for those wins. They're all part of your journey, and they matter.

Now, let's talk about setbacks. Yeah, they happen. Life's not always sunshine and rainbows. But here's the deal: setbacks can be opportunities for growth. When you hit a bump in the road, take a moment to reflect on what you learned. Celebrate the resilience it took to get back up and keep going. That's a win in itself!

And speaking of setbacks, let's not forget the power of gratitude. When you take time to appreciate what you have, it shifts your perspective. Instead of focusing on what's missing, you start to see the abundance around you. Gratitude and celebration go hand in hand. So, take a moment each day to jot down a few things you're grateful for. It's a simple practice that can have a huge impact on your mindset.

As we wrap up this celebration chat, remember that your journey is uniquely yours. Embrace every twist and turn, every victory and setback. Recognizing your progress isn't just a nice idea; it's essential for your growth.

Reflecting on your successes keeps you grounded and connected to your purpose. And those small celebrations? They're the fuel that'll keep your fire burning bright.

So go ahead, take a moment today to celebrate. Whether it's a dance party in your living room, a quiet moment of gratitude, or a mini-adventure, honor your journey. You're doing amazing things, and you deserve to recognize that. Keep climbing, keep celebrating, and watch as abundance flows into your life like a river after a rainstorm. You've got this!

Life's a journey, folks. So buckle up, enjoy the ride, and don't forget to celebrate along the way.

Index